Jacques MARÉCHAL

HASTINGS
BATTLE FOR A KINGDOM

1066

Translated from french by Jennifer Meyniel

General editor Yann Kervran

HISTOIRE & COLLECTIONS

Summary

Introduction

2006

For this second edition of the battle re-enactment, the organisers were able to reunite more than 2000 re-enactors in costume from the 11th century. Volunteers came with their own arms, from all over Europe, as well as Australia and America. According to official figures, there were 132 archers, 91 cavalry, and 1279 infantry, a total of 1500 combatants. In addition to these figures, there were 491 non combatants, some of whom were children. This figure represents approximately a tenth of the number of people who actually took part in the battle in 1066. The organisers were extremely vigilant as regards the authenticity of the costumes, and only re-enactors who wore costumes which were historically realistic were allowed to participate at the event. All of the participants had to ensure that the colour of their costumes represented their social position. Only the rich could wear red, blue, green or bright shades of fabrics, jewellery or embroidered clothes. The poorer had to settle for earthy colours, brown, cream or un-dyed fabrics, and inexpensive decorative details. Modern fabrics and objects were forbidden, as was the wearing of glasses and watches. The re-enactors had to choose either to be Norman, Fle- mish, French, Breton or Saxon, and had to comply with the dress code used by these people in the 11th century.

1066

On the 5th of January 1066, the king of England, Edward the Confessor died. Harold, the Earl of Wessex was crowned the following day. News of this event outraged all of the lords from Western Europe, especially William, Duke of Normandy, who had a claim to the throne. He immediately began to prepare an impressive military expedition.

During the first seven months of 1066, William formed an army and rallied together volunteers from Normandy, Brittany, Flanders and Bourgogne….He assembled more than 800 ships to sail across the English Channel.

While preparing for the invasion, William pleaded his cause with the Pope Alexander II, who gave him Vatican approval, and permission to fly the papal banner.

On the 28th of September, William landed on English shores near to Hastings. He knew that the English army had moved more than 350km up north, which gave him plenty of time to take position. Alerted, Harold's troops began, despite their exhaustion after their battle at Stamford Bridge against Harold Hardrada, to move down south to face the Normans. William, who had learned of his ally's bitter defeat, immediately believed that Harold, despite his victory, would be weakened. The Duke knew that if he wanted to win the battle, he would have to rapidly confront his enemy. He had to force him to attack.

Location

The re-enactment took place at Senlac Hill, the very battlefield where in 1066 the battle was fought between William II, the Duke of Normandy and Harold II, the King of England. The hill is at the entrance of the present day town of Battle, eight kilometres north of Hastings which is on the coast. As a backdrop, there are the ruins of the abbey which was built by William the Conqueror at the end of the 11th century to commemorate the battle, and in memory of the large number of troops who died on that day.

Organisation

The associations "The Vikings" and "English Heritage" joined forces to organise the re-enactment of the Battle of Hastings. This international event took place on the historic site of the battle, and the organisers placed emphasis on the authenticity of the re-enactors' appearance. Two battles which lasted approximately two hours were organised, one on the Saturday 14th October, day of the 940th anniversary of the battle, and one on Sunday 15th.

The encampments

William the Conqueror had brought a large quantity of running supplies. Incidentally there is a scene on the "Bayeux Tapestry" which depicts a meal time. While the Lords ate at a table with a table cloth and their food served in quality tableware by servants, the combatants, the archers and their companions had to manage as best they could: They ate on the ground, on their shields or directly from the cooking pot. Two manuscripts from that era describe the tents: two vertical poles held a horizontal rod which supported the canvas which was held taut by pegs. The Anglo Saxon encampment would have been very similar, although there is no written extract from the era to confirm this.

A Norman guard.

A Norman banner
with the inscription
« Dex aïe » meaning
« God help us »

*On the right hand page,
Norman encampment.*

Repairs to a shield

Transport of equipment for the battle

On the right hand page
Making a coin

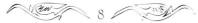

*Common soldiers had no other
choice but to eat sitting on the
ground, or on their shields.*

*It was common to see entire families in the Saxon encampment, because,
for the Fyrd at least, they were not far from home.*

The tents couldn't accommodate all of the combatants and their equipment. Some had to sleep outdoors.

The men at arms were accompanied by attendants who prepared their meals, tended to their horses, and repaired weapons.

Most of the Saxon
nobles had a beard
and long hair.

The Norman Lord was easily recognisable by his haircut.

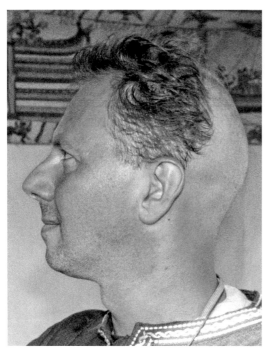

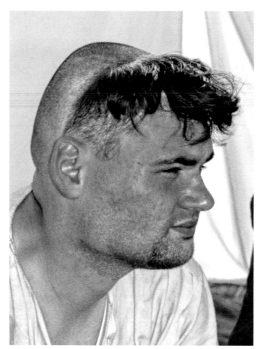

the Norman Lord was easily recognisable by his haircut and his battle mace.

Opposite page, in general the Lords ate at a table, and were served food in quality tableware by servants.

Opposite page, below, Some of the Norman lords brought sheir wives and children with them.

The wealthier Norman lords brought servants and priests with them.

Armour

The most efficient form of protection was the hauberk which was a coat of mail reaching down to the knees. It was made up of thousands of small loops of iron woven together. Other forms of armour were also worn, such as ring mail, made up of small metallic scales sewn onto a fabric. The gambeson was probably the most common form of armour. It was a jacket made from linen or from hemp, stuffed with wool, horse hair or scrap cloth.

Above,
a Norman soldier busy
preparing himself for battle.

On the left,
a squire repairing the chain mail on his knight's hauberk.

"The most efficient form of protection was the hauberk which was a coat of mail reaching to the knees."

Chain mail hose (trousers), a very rare form of armour at that period.

Norman lord recognizable by his battle mace.

On the left hand page
A squire repairing the chain mail to his knight's hauberk.

The helmets

The "Bayeux tapestry" depicts one type of head protection, the conical helmet with a nose guard which is often called the "Norman helmet", even though at that period, it was worn by all of the soldiers from Western Europe. It was generally made of four iron triangles riveted onto four upright pieces in the shape of a cross, and secured together along the lower edge by an iron ring, on which the nose guard was also fixed. On the helmets belonging to poorer soldiers, the" boiled leather" replaced one or several parts of the helmet.

Through close observation of the tapestry, it is possible to discern that at least one helmet has been forged from one single piece which was unusual because this technique requires an expertise that few blacksmiths possessed at that period.

Group of Norman troops preparing for battle. Some are wearing a hauberk and others a gambeson.

In the right, helmet made from one single piece, which was unusual at that period due to the technical expertise required to make it.

On the right,
an ordinary helmet.

Two conical helmets with nose protection.
The one on the left is entirely made from metal,
whereas the one on the right has parts made from
"boiled leather."

On archer's helmet which is made entirely
from "boiled leather" and has no nose guard.

The most common type of helmet.

On the left,
a lord's helmet with gilded bronze detail, and engravings.

Opposite page and above,
two Norman soldiers.

Norman lord wearing a chain mail hose (trousers), a very rare form of armour at that period.

The shields

The entire Norman army and a large part of the Saxon army used kite shaped or almond shaped shields during this period. The shield was made from two wooden strips joined together, stuck with animal skin adhesive and covered with leather which made the shield more solid. The other type of shield was round and it was made in the same way. It was used by part of the Saxon army. The designs on them were not blazons, as they did not yet exist.

*Opposite page and above,
a kite shaped or almond shaped shield. Some still have an umbo in the middle, a small iron boss to protect the hand.*

*Below,
a group of Saxons with round shields. All of their shields had an umbo in the middle and ornamental Celt decorations.*

Saxon soldier recognizable by his great axe.

The sword

The sword was the most prestigious weapon for knights and warriors during the Middle Ages. It could be held in one hand, and was used during hand to hand combat. Up until the 12th century it measured slightly more than 90cm in length, and it had a two-edged sharp blade with a relatively rounded head. This suggests that it was a weapon used mainly to deliver powerful blows (with the blade edge) and not to strike (with the blade tip). It was principally the shape of the pommel (the handle) that gave the sword its originality.

Hand to hand combat.

The sword was
the most prestigious
weapon for knights and
warriors during
the Middle Ages.

*The cavalry used the sword when
the enemy was not sheltered
behind a shield wall.*

The lance

The lance was the most common weapon. The infantry had long lances measuring at least two metres. It could be used with one hand for a thrusting strike (with the head).It could also be thrown like a javelin. As for the cavalry, the spear was rarely longer than three metres, and it was occasionally decorated with a banner. They used it as a throwing weapon, but they generally blocked it under their armpits, against their bodies, a technique that became widespread later on, and known as the "underarm couched lance charge."

This group of mounted soldiers still uses the lance the old fashioned way; that is holding it like a javelin.

*On the right and left,
in these two photos, it is easy to compare the different lengths
between the infantry's lance and the cavalry's lance.*

The battle axe

The great battle axe or the Danish axe was mainly used by the Saxons, and in particular by the housecarls who were well trained soldiers devoted to their lord. The axe measured as long as two metres, and it was a two handed weapon used to deliver devastating blows in the Norman ranks. Some axes with short handles were also used by both armies.

On the left,
a Norman mounted soldier with a battle axe.

In the hands of the housecarls, the great Danish axe with the long handle wreaked havoc in the Norman ranks.

A housecarl with a great Danish axe.

The bow

The bow was most certainly the least expensive weapon, and the easiest to make, but one which required a good deal of practice. The archer was generally lightly clothed to allow for rapid movement. In addition to his bow, the archer also had a quiver to carry his arrows, and a knife for hand to hand combat. During a pitched battle, the archers fired their arrows into the air, which gave them a parabolic trajectory before landing on the enemy troops.

Arrows with nock and fletchings.

This group of archers clearly illustrates their lack of body armour or any other weapon.

The arbalest

Although there is no representation on the "Bayeux tapestry", mediaeval sources document the use of the arbalest during the battle. Their arrows could be fired directly, which, coupled with the plunging archers' arrows, were fearsome. The weapon was made of a wooden bow, with a wooden piece to fix the bow (the stock) and a mechanism used to draw the string tight (the nut) to release the arrow (the trigger) and to tighten the bow. The short arrows fired by the arbalest were known as quarrels. The arbalest was powerful and precise, a deadly weapon.

Opposite page,
the first versions of the
arbalest appeared during
this period. The bow was
made from yew wood and
it had no specific system to
draw it tight.

« The arbalest was power-
ful and precise, a deadly
weapon »

The arbalester aimed at his
target, firing directly which
had lethal consequences.

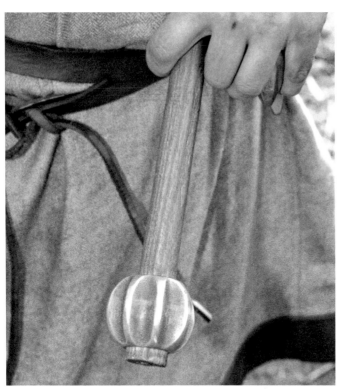

The battle mace

Primarily, it was a symbol of leadership, reserved for the high ranking lords. However, it was also an offensive weapon with a handle and a blunt head at the other end. Originally it was a mere piece of wood with the stump attached; but subsequently the blunt head was made of metal. Blows delivered by the mace could easily smash a skull or a limb even through a coat of mail.

*Opposite page,
a troop leader conveys orders
with the use of his commander's club.*

Battle axe, partly made from metal.

William shows his commander's club to his troops.

The Saxon army

Harold's army, composed of seven to eight thousand infantrymen, took up position on the ridge of Senlac Hill. The men were aligned over 800 metres, and they were split into ten or twelve tight ranks. Harold, and his two brothers, Gurth and Lewine, the Earls of Estanglie and Essex were in the centre. They were protected by the housecarls, professional warriors who used the Danish axe and wore a hauberk and a helmet. The fringes were reserved for members of the Fyrd, who were a collection of free men aged between 16 and 60; they were grouped by their place of origin. They were generally led by a thegn (semi professional warrior who held his estate on the understanding that in times of war he would fight.) In reality they were ill prepared peasants, ready to do anything for their lord. They were poorly equipped, armed with javelins or slings. The tactic was simple. This wall of soldiers had to remain in place and hold back Norman assaults, in order to weaken them before the counter attack.

« The saxon army. There are nearly seven hundred combatants in this photo, wich is ten times fewer than during the actual battle »

Harold II, King of England

Born in 1022, Harold became the Earl of Wessex in 1053. This county, which at that period represented a third of England, meant that he became England's most powerful man after the King. When Edward the Confessor died on the 5th of January 1066, Harold declared that Edward had promised him the throne while on his deathbed. The Witan (an assembly of noblemen who governed the kingdom) approved his coronation, which took place the following day. Killed at Hastings, he was the last Saxon king of England.

Harold with his brother Lewine, the Earl of Essex.

Harold II,
king of England.

Harold arrives
at the battlefield
leading his troops

The Norman army

The Normans were nearly as numerous as the Saxons. William had separated his army into three divisions: the Bretons on the left, the Normans in the centre, and the Flemish, with mercenaries from all over France on the extreme right. Each division was split into three sections: the archers at the front, the infantry in the centre, and the cavalry at the rear. In total there were fifteen hundred archers, nearly four thousand five hundred infantrymen and approximately two thousand cavalrymen.

The cavalry was the army's major asset, because during the 11th century it was considered as the best in the Christendom. Indeed, it could charge in tightly packed groups, carry out strategic retreats, and obey orders given by their commanders who fought at their head. They were also skilled at regrouping during a battle. To carry out these manoeuvres, the Normans organised themselves into conrois, groups of twenty to thirty cavalrymen who charged in two lines. Ten conrois formed a bataille.

On the right, some Norman cavalrymen.

William II, Duke of Normandy

Born around 1028 in Falaise, he was known successively as William the bastard, William II of Normandy, William the Conqueror, and finally as William I King of England after his coronation in Westminster Abbey on Christmas Day 1066. When his cousin, Edward the Confessor died, he made his claim to the throne, declaring that as Edward had no child, he had been chosen as heir. He accused Harold of betrayal, persuaded the Pope Alexander II to excommunicate him, and then he carefully prepared his invasion.

The three sections of a Norman division, at the front the archers, in the centre the infantry and at the rear the cavalry.

William II,
Duc of Normandy.

William charges leading his men.

The battle

The arrival of Norman cavalrymen.

The battle of Hastings began on the morning of the 14th October, at approximately 9am.

benediction of the Normans before the battle

Norman troops arrive.

Saxon troops arrive.

On the right,
benediction of
the Saxons before
the battle

The battle began with a massive archery offensive on the Saxons.

*Above,
the arrows fired by the Normans
fail to penetrate the Saxon shield
wall.*

*The Norman infantrymen were then
sent to the Saxon shield wall, which
had not been weakened by the
archers.*

*On the left,
the Norman cavalrymen take up
position for battle.*

Arrogant Norman soldier reacts to the English provocation.

Taillefer, the Duke's court jester, over arrogantly charges the enemy alone. He causes the battle's first victims, by killing two Saxon soldiers. He is rapidly surrounded, dismounted and his throat cut.

Above,
The majority of the Norman infantry is now engaged in the battle.

The Saxons fight the" Celtic" way; namely by looking for one to one combat, which is not an effective method against battle hardened combatants who fight as a group.

The French, the Picard and the Flemish contingents initially have to climb a short slope to confront their enemies.

The two armies come into contact.

The Saxon lines falter but they do not break.

The successive
Norman infantry
charges fail to pene-
trate the shield wall.

Some groups of
Saxon soldiers
launch a counter
attack.

Tthe left wing of the Norman army collapses and retreats in chaos, causing a large number of Saxons from the right wing to pursue them, impatient to put an end to the fight.

The Saxons encouraged by what they believe to be the Norman rout, begin to attack the cavalry.

Successive cavalry charges with no respite for the enemy.

The fight begins again on the left with another cavalry attack on the Saxon wall.

The cavalry now attack the Saxon wall from all sides.

William, still alive takes off his helmet and gallops around the battlefield to rally the Norman and French contingents, and to re launch them into the battle..

« As soon as one group of cavaliers accomplishes their mission, another group replaces them »

The Norman cavalry charges and throws projectiles without taking part in hand to hand combat.

This tactic begins to exhaust the Saxons, and gaps in the wall become apparent

By the end of the afternoon, the Saxon shield wall has completely collapsed.

Opposite page,
William decides to put an end to the battle, and he directly attacks Harold's headquarters.

The Saxons who broke ranks were massacred in a matter of seconds by the Norman cavalry.

King Harold died
during the battle,
as well as his
brothers and the
most important Anglo
Saxon lords.

The end of the final assault on King Harold's close guards

The Normans shout victory.

William becomes the Conqueror and the ruler of the kingdom.

*Opposite page,
with no remaining opposition, the Duke
of Normandy was to be crowned King of England
on the 25th December 1066 at Westminster.*

The exhausted soldiers rest and nurse their wounded.

It had been a long day...

Acknowledgements

The author would particularly like to thank:

Mrs Emily Burns from the association "English Heritage" and her fellow colleagues.

Mrs Sandie Gillbanks and the members of the association "The Vikings".

Mrs Heather Fletcher, Anne Beaujean and Claire Maréchal,

Mr Marc Goosens and Benoit Maréchal, As well as Nikon Belgium for their help.

All the associations which participated in this re-enactment: AD Historical Interpretation, The Albini Household, Anmod Dracan, Les Arbalétriers Flamands, Arcieri nel Tempo, The Association of the Centre of Slavs and Vikings Wolin, L'Association Guerre et Chevalerie, Bowmen of the Kingswood, Britannia, British Plate Armour Society, C.H.E.S., Canes Vivarensis, Christophus, Colchester Roman Society, Comitatus, La Compagnia del Fiore D'Argento, La Compagnia della Rosa e della Spada, La Compagnie de la Branche Rouge, La Compagnie de la Licorne, Les Compagnons du Cerf, Company Of Chivalry, Complutum, La Confrérie Normande, Conquest, Dewarenne Household, Druzyna grodu trzyglowa, East Kent Historical Organisation (EKHO), Eldrimnir, Elvegrimarne, Equites Digni, ERA, Far Isles Medieval Society, Fingal Living History Society, Franco Flemish Contingent, The Free Company, Gael agus Gall, De Gentsche Ghesellen, La Geste Médiévale, Grásida, Great Northwood Bowmen, Les Guerriers d'Avalon, Hag'Dik, Halsingarna, Hasteinn, Havkhersar, Henrys Men, Holderness, The Household, Jabberwooky e.V. Karlsruhe, The Jomsvikings, Knights in Battle, Die Landen van Herwaerts Over, Leofwine's Hearth troop, La Maisnie Penthièvre, Medieval Siege Society, The Mercenaries of Midgard, Meridies Northmannorum, Die Milzener e.V, Nordhere, Nordmannia, Northland Mercenaries, Odinsvi, Paladins of Chivalry, Raven's Wing Vikings, Regia Angelorum, Rimmug gur, Rudhaborg Ulfar, Samhain Welsh Medieval Society, SCA, Shields of the Shattered Isles, Silver Wolf, SkŒnska PilbŒgegillet, Slavians, Solbjerg Glima, South Rus, Stichting Armae, Swords of Dalriada, Le Temps d'un Rêve,Teutonica, The Traditional Archery Society of Ireland, UCO Medieval Society, The University of Birmingham Battle re-enactment Society, Uppsala Medieval Society, Vennerne, Vigrid, Vikingekampgruppen Odd, The Vikings, Vikings Finland, Vikings of Middle England, Vikings North America, Viking Society of Run, V'kverir, Vinhold Lance, Walhalla, Wolfguard, Wulfingas 450 -550 AD, Wychwood Warriors, Xiazeca Druzyna and those whose names and addresses are unknown.

During the battle re-enactment in 2006, there was a minute of silence, in memory of all the victims who fell during battle in 1066.

Design and lay-out Denis Gandilhon, Magali Masselin, Jean-Marie Mongin and Antoine Poggioli based upon the author's work.

A book published by

Histoire et Collections

SA au capital de 182 938,82 €

5, avenue de la République F-75541 Paris Cedex 11 FRANCE

Telephone: +33(1) 40 21 18 20 - Fax: +33(1) 47 00 51 11

www.histoireetcollections.fr

Pictures integrated by Studio A&C.

Printed by Zure, Spain, European Union.

August 2009

ISBN : 978-2-35250-082-7

Publisher's number : 35250

© Histoire & Collections 2009.